A PORT THROUGH TIME

ILLUSTRATED BY STEVE NOON

WRITTEN BY DR ANNE MILLARD

DK

London, New York, Melbourne,
Munich, and Delhi

Project Editor Jenny Finch
Art Editor Sheila Collins
Senior Editor Francesca Baines
Managing Editor Linda Esposito
Managing Art Editor Diane Thistlethwaite
Publishing Manager Andrew Macintyre
Category Publisher Laura Buller
Picture Researcher Myriam Megharbi, Rob Nunn
DK Picture Researcher Rose Horridge, Claire Bowers
Production Controller Seyhan Esen-Yagmurlu
DTP Designer Siu Chan

First published in Great Britain in 2006
by Dorling Kindersley Limited,
80 Strand, London, WC2R 0RL

A CIP catalogue for this book is available
from the British Library.

ISBN-13: 978-1-40531-267-7
ISBN-10: 1-4053-1267-X

Colour reproduction by Wyndeham-Icon, UK
Printed and bound by Tien Wah Press, Malaysia

Discover more at
www.dk.com

CONTENTS

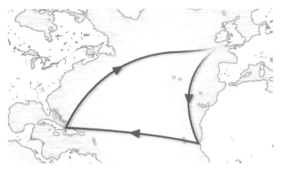

THE STORY OF A PORT

About 10,000 years ago, the Ice Age ended and new plants and animals spread across Europe, followed by human beings who quickly adapted to the warmer conditions. Our story is set on the coast, along the sheltered shores of a large natural bay, and explains why this special place developed over time into a thriving port. It focuses on the different ships and goods that passed through the port and the trading links forged with peoples and places all around the world. The story follows the fortunes of the port and the people who lived here, through good times and bad, and shows how it changed through history as needs, tastes, and opportunities altered.

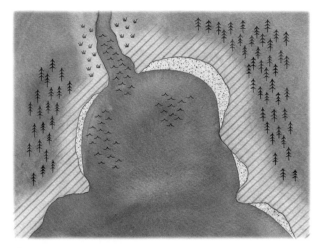

AERIAL VIEW OF THE BAY

KEY

 WOODLAND   BEACH

 FIRM GROUND   MARSHLAND

NATURAL HARBOUR

The water is shallow along the shoreline, but it is very deep further out in the bay. Marshes spread around the river mouth and many birds live in its reeds. The land slopes up from the shore, and on this higher ground a thick forest grows, which is home to many animals and birds.

STONE-AGE HUNTERS (AROUND 9,000 YEARS AGO)

Every summer, a tribe of hunter-gatherers camps on the shores of the bay. It is a good spot, sheltered from any storms. There is fresh water to drink and birds and their eggs to eat. The tribespeople hunt game and gather plants and berries in the forest. They fish from canoes made of hollowed-out tree trunks and gather shellfish. In winter, they move inland and trade highly prized shells for other goods from the tribes they meet there.

EARLY FARMERS (AROUND 5,000 YEARS AGO)

When knowledge of farming spread across Europe, a tribe settled by the bay where their ancestors had camped. Besides raising crops and animals, they still do some hunting and a lot of fishing. Representatives of a tribe from further inland sail down the river bringing top-quality flints from their mine to trade for dried fish, reed baskets, and other goods. Others from a third tribe living a long way down the coast come by boat to join the trading.

4

BRONZE-AGE JEWELLERY
Archaeologists have found examples of skilfully crafted jewellery – such as these gold bracelets – made by smiths in the Bronze Age.

IRON-AGE FLAGON
As well as practical tools and weapons, iron-age smiths made objects of great beauty. This bronze flagon, decorated with coral, was used for pouring wine, beer, or mead at feasts. It would have been a valuable trade item.

IRON AGE (AROUND 2,300 YEARS AGO)

People have discovered how to work iron, which is much harder than bronze. Some goods are traded right across Europe over land, by rivers, and along the coasts. The bay is popular because it provides sheltered moorings. The villagers have built a quay, made of rubble enclosed in wood, where larger ships can moor. Occasionally, they are even visited by adventurers from the Mediterranean world who exchange wine and luxury goods for furs, amber, cloth, slaves, and any metals the villagers will sell.

BRONZE AGE (AROUND 3,500 YEARS AGO)

People have discovered how to work gold and how to make bronze from copper and tin. The village has two highly skilled metal smiths – a father and son. Traders come long distances to buy their tools, weapons, and jewels. Increased trade makes the village and its chief rich and respected. They now control land right around the bay. Our villagers also travel long distances to buy tin and special hard stones that make querns, used to grind grain. They also mount expeditions to quarry large slabs of stone to build monuments honouring their gods and goddesses and their dead ancestors.

WHERE IS HE?

This is a very unlucky and accident-prone man – and so are all his descendants. Trace the disasters that befall them through the centuries. They are easy to spot because they are all dressed in red, yellow, and green. To check you've found them turn to page 32.

UNDER ROMAN RULE (C. 150 CE)

The Romans have conquered the port, bringing with them Roman laws and customs. The port is governed from the Basilica, which also houses the law courts, and people worship Roman gods and goddesses. Many foreigners have settled here, and exotic goods are imported from distant parts of the Roman Empire. In turn, local goods are exported, including grain, wool, silver, slaves, and even bears and wolves destined for the arena in Rome.

Can you see who has stepped in elephant dung?

Marble is imported from Italy to decorate important buildings.

Temple

Greek teacher

Public speaker

Basilica

Forum (market)

Cloth merchant

Papyrus store

Apartments

Apartments

Slaves escaping

Glassware

Ivory

Jeweller

Greek doctor

Merchant's house

Spices

Olive oil

Olives

Shrine

Furs

Wolf

Wine

Bear

Litter

Syrian merchant

Wool for export

Missionary

Merchant

Celts

6

Local traders have brought salt from along the coast to sell at the market.

Lions and other wild beasts are imported to entertain the crowds in the local arena.

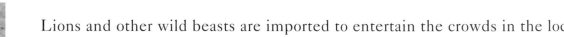

Arena

Metal smith

Workshops

Fishermen's nets

Soldiers

Boat building

Potter

Washing clothes

Trading ship

Warehouses

Spanish horses

Spanish lawyer

Timber

Patrolling the coast

Grain

Grain for export

Bronze worker

Guarding silver

Treadmill crane

Pottery

...ern

Escaping lion

Silk

Jars of fish pickle sauce

Spices

Ship carrying exports

Salt

Local fishermen

Furs

Grain

7

Slaves about to be sent to Rome try to escape from their guards.

Find the clumsy slave who is getting a beating.

Port officials keep a record of all imports and exports so they can be taxed.

This ship has brought expensive treasures from the East, such as silk and spices.

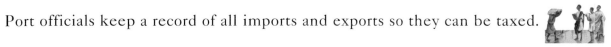

A New Start (c. 950)

Many foreign invaders have settled in the port and mixed with the local people. Christianity, which became the official religion of the late Roman period, has survived the fall of the Roman Empire. The Church is becoming rich and powerful. A lord governs the area for the king, and a chief runs the port's day-to-day affairs. The lord charges the people taxes in return for protection against Viking raiders and hostile neighbouring lords. Most trade is local, though some exotic goods are imported for the very rich. The main exports are grain, fish, honey, furs, wool, and salt.

Fishing

Wedding party ship

Jetty

Imported ivory and wine

Wool

Pilgrims

Drying fish

Making barrels

Dyeing cloth

Sail

Thatchers

Cloth

Baskets

Toilet

Leather wares

Jewellery

Dried foods

Bead maker

Honey

Ivory and bone

Grinding grain

Salting fish

Glass beads

Fish

Fisherwomen

Grain

Apple thief!

8

Fort

Defensive wall

Boat building

Viking trader

Smith

Warship guarding the coast

Merchant's ship

Chief's hall

Wine and grain

Salt making

Tannery

Pottery

Falcons

Furs

Store

Stained glass window

Carpenter

Loom

Wine

Spinning

Drying fish

Scales

Slave market

Glass

Furs

Iron weapons

Silk

Axe heads

Quernstones

Bronze

Church

Wool

Local merchant

Priest

Missionaries

9

 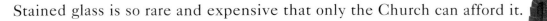

Christian missionaries are setting off to convert pagans abroad.

How many ruined Roman buildings can you see?

WIDENING HORIZONS (C. 1190)

It is the morning of the weekly market, and people have come from the surrounding countryside to sell their produce. The port is ruled by a lord, but the merchants and craftsmen have started to form guilds and become more powerful. Religious wars, called Crusades, are being fought in the Middle East, bringing people into contact with exotic goods like sugar and spices. The Italian ports of Venice and Genoa control the trade in these goods, which are very expensive. Most trade is local, with grain, fur, honey, and wool exported to neighbouring countries.

What has made the pigs stampede?

Christian Crusaders are off to win back the Holy Land from the Muslim Saracens.

Boats for coastal and river trade

Tannery

Dyeing cloth

Wheelwright

Harness maker

Smithy

Leather worker

Sharpening tools

Logs

Carpenter's workshop

Stained glass windows

Tapestry

Candlemaker

Moneylender

Anxious clients

Store

Washerwoman

Grain

Crusaders

Crusaders' soldiers

Priest

Dancing bear

Ribbons

Stave-fight

Stocks

Drinking water for sale

Animals for sale

Honey

Wealthy pilgrims

Pilgrims

10

A ship has arrived from Venice with silk, pepper, and raisins from the East.   The lord has left his castle to check on the bailiff, his representative in the port.

Local farmers have brought vegetables to sell at the market.   Find the nobleman who has just been hit by a football.

Venetian ship

Silk

Pepper

Raisins

Barrel-maker

Ivory

Merchant's house

Loading wool for export

Loading Crusaders' horses

Loading Crusaders' supplies

Crusaders' ship

Potter

Stone

Kilns

Bathhouse

Baker

Bailiff's house

Weaver's house

Inn

Packing wool

Toilet

Inn's stables

Drunken brawl

Ironmonger's shop

Baskets

Packhorses

Lady's coach

Cheese

Merchant

Eggs

Pottery

Beggar

Birds

Vegetables

Bread

Fleeces

Cloth

Fish

Bone

Fish

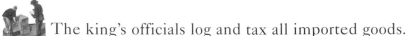 The king's officials log and tax all imported goods.  A Portuguese captain plans to sail around Africa to trade directly with the East, bypassing the Italians and Turks.

FUN OF THE FAIR (C. 1450)

The lord has sold a charter for the port, and it is now run by the mayor and a council made up of rich merchants and guild masters. They hold an annual fair, and foreign merchants from across Europe flock to buy and sell. For local people, it is very profitable – and great fun! Italians still control trade with the East, and have invented banking, opening branches all over Europe.

Lord's castle

Guildhall

Shops

Boat building

Timber

Flemish ship

Scandinavian ship

Venetian ship

Crane

Venetian merchant galley

Tar

Italian armour

German ship

Local grain

French wine

Loading goods for river trade

Venetian ship

Bringing goods ashore

Maps

Sailors

Travelling dentist

Ferryman

Sick sailor

Piper

Dance

Portuguese ship

Spanish swords

Clerk

Grain

Cannon

Local cheeses

Spinning tops

Fire-eater

Cockfight

Cutp

12

 The cannon is a new weapon that has been developed, and it is about to change warfare for ever. Port officials hope that this sick sailor doesn't have the plague.

Aeroplane

Oil depot

Radio room

Oil sheikhs

Seasick

Warships

Gangster and bodyguards   Italian count   American millionairess

Sugar

Tanks for export

Tobacco

Soldiers

Maid

Radio reporter

Reporters

Customs men

Typists

Film stars

Police

Manager

Foreman

Soup kitchen

Movie mogul

Busker

Bellboy

Luggage

Wine supplies

Secretary

Unemployed dockers

25

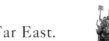

BUSINESS AND PLEASURE (PRESENT DAY)

Multinational companies now control the majority of the port's trade, and container shipping has streamlined the transport of goods. The port has a new marina and many new leisure facilities, as ordinary people have more time and money to enjoy themselves. People are also more environmentally aware, and campaign to protect wildlife and historic buildings.

Multinational company

University

Museum

Hotel

Communications' mast

Construction workers

Caught smoking!

Offices

Shopping mall

CCTV

Café

Checking delivery

Demonstrators

Office

Old guildhall

Satellite dishes

Developers' plans

Imported fruit

Press

School party

Local radio station

TV crew

Mobile phone

For export

26

Demonstrators

Texting

How many new ways to communicate can you spot?

Old warehouses have been converted into a shopping mall.

  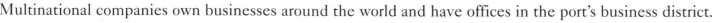

Air-sea rescue helicopter

Grain silos

Nature reserve

Oil refinery

Cruise liner

Luxury apartments

Container ship

Satellite navigation

Computerized bridge

Captain

Visiting foreign warship

Cabin

Using a laptop

Fishermen's boats

Jacuzzi

Dining room

Luxury yacht

Ferry

Jet-skis

Marina

Smugglers

Customs' launch

Illegal immigrant

Immigration officers

Sniffer dog

27

Planes carry passengers and perishable goods much quicker than ships.

Can you spot what one unlucky angler has caught?

A WORLD OF TRADE

Over the centuries, traders have often proved to be explorers, discovering new lands as well as new goods. Trade went on to shape the world, as new ports were established, existing ports grew, and some countries were colonized.

ALEXANDRIA This Egyptian city was founded in 332 BCE by Alexander the Great. It grew into a centre of learning and trade, and became one of the great cities of his empire. Around 299 BCE, work began on a huge lighthouse just outside the busy port. Called the Pharos, the lighthouse was one of the Seven Wonders of the World.

AMSTERDAM The capital of Holland was at its height during the 17th and 18th centuries when the country was a great sea power, and the Dutch East India Company controlled trade with the East Indies and South Africa. From the 16th century to the present day, Amsterdam has been a centre for the diamond trade.

ARCHANGEL Until 1703, the only Russian trading port was Archangel on the Arctic coast. Although icebound half the year, icebreakers now make access possible and it is a busy port today. Major exports are wood and timber products.

BORDEAUX One of the most valuable commodities in the medieval period was wine. France was a major wine producer and the port of Bordeaux, on the Atlantic coast, was the chief exporting city.

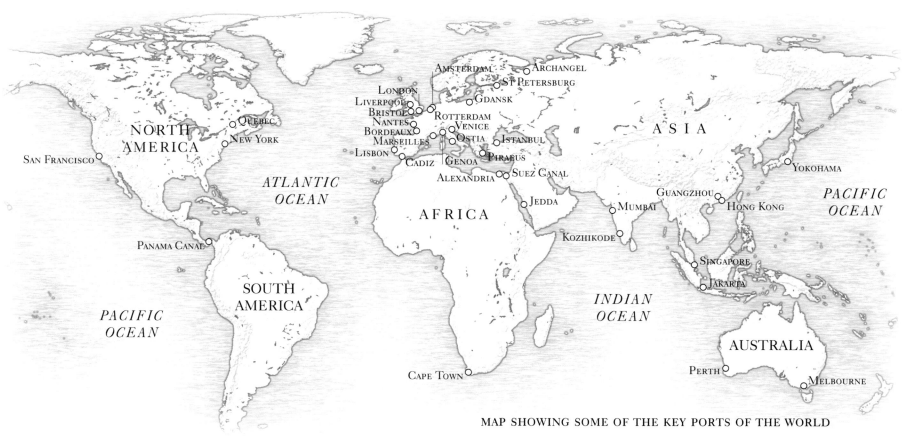

MAP SHOWING SOME OF THE KEY PORTS OF THE WORLD

CADIZ Situated on a headland, there has been a port on the Atlantic coast of Spain at Cadiz since 1100 BCE. In the 16th century, Cadiz became the base for Spanish treasure ships during the conquest of the New World.

CAPE TOWN On the southwestern tip of South Africa, Cape Town was founded in 1652 as a supply station for the Dutch East India Company. It is still an important port today, exporting gold, diamonds, and fruit.

GDANSK The Polish port of Gdansk lies on the Baltic Sea and was formerly known as Danzig. The port joined the Hanseatic League in the 13th century, which was an alliance of trading cities around the Baltic that became the most important economic power in the medieval period.

GENOA The city of Genoa in Italy prospered under Roman rule, and again during the Crusades, as soldiers and traders passed through the port on their way to and from the Holy Land. It went on to become a powerful trade and banking centre, and today Genoa is Italy's chief port.

HONG KONG Hong Kong Island, on the southeast coast of China, became a British colony in the mid-19th century and was occupied under an arrangement that ended in 1997, when it was returned to China. Its position, on the edge of China, has made the port an important centre of trade and banking between the East and West.

ISTANBUL The Turkish port of Istanbul lies on a channel, called the Bosporus, that links the Mediterranean Sea to the Black Sea and Asia beyond. It was founded in 660 BCE as Byzantium, and in 330 CE was renamed Constantinople when it became the capital of the Eastern Roman Empire. The port's rich history and position on the edge of two continents gives it an exciting and exotic mix of peoples and cultures.

JAKARTA On the island of Java, Jakarta is the largest city in Indonesia. It was founded in 1691 by the Dutch and was at that time called Batavia. It was the centre of trade for spices such as nutmeg, cinnamon, cloves, and pepper, as well as tea, silk, and Chinese porcelain.

JEDDA Jedda, or Jidda, lies on the Red Sea in Saudi Arabia. For hundreds of years, it has been a key port for Muslims from all over the world making the pilgrimage, or hajj, to Mecca.

PEPPERCORNS

CINNAMON STICKS

NUTMEGS

CLOVES

PRECIOUS SPICES

For thousands of years, spices have been highly prized. Once, cinnamon was more valuable than gold, and pepper so precious it was used as money. Spices became important in Europe in the Middle Ages for flavouring meat that had been preserved in salt. The huge profits to be made from the spice trade drove European merchants west to find new routes to India.

KOZHIKODE Until the 19th century, Calicut, now called Kozhikode, was the main port of southern India. It first became a centre for trade with Arab merchants, and later with merchants from Europe. It is now important for trade in timber, coconuts, spices, tea, and coffee.

GOLD ORE

GOLDRUSH
Until gold was discovered nearby in 1848, San Francisco was just a small town on the West Coast of America. With the arrival of thousands of fortune hunters, it quickly grew into a bustling port. A few years later, the discovery of gold in Australia led to the boom of the ports of Melbourne and Perth.

LISBON The Portuguese capital has been an important trading centre for thousands of years. In the 15th century, explorers set off from Lisbon in search of India. In 1731, a terrible earthquake almost completely destroyed the city.

MARSEILLES The oldest city in France, Marseilles was settled by Greeks from the East around 660 BCE. The port lies on the Mediterranean Sea, and during the Crusades became a centre of trade as many pilgrims and soldiers passed through on their way to the Holy Land. Today, Marseilles is one of France's most important seaports and a major industrial city.

MUMBAI The main port and industrial centre of India is Mumbai, on the Arabian Sea. It lies on seven islands around a natural deep-water harbour. In the 16th century, Portugal controlled this area of India and the city was known as Bombay, Portuguese for "good bay". But from the 17th century, until Indian independence in 1947, it was controlled by Britain.

NEW YORK Founded by the Dutch in 1624 as New Amsterdam, New York was renamed by the British in 1664. It lies on the East Coast of the USA. In the 18th century, it became a centre for banking and the Stock Exchange, and by 1840 New York had become the leading port in the USA. In the 19th century, huge numbers of immigrants from Europe passed through the port on their way to seek their fortune in America.

OSTIA This ancient Italian city, at the mouth of the River Tiber, was the port of the Roman capital. It was at its height of activity in the first century CE, as goods from all over the Roman Empire passed through the port.

PANAMA CANAL The Panama Canal links the Pacific and Atlantic Oceans. It was opened in 1914 and is 82 km (51 miles) long. Its construction meant ships could avoid the dangerous waters off Cape Horn, at the tip of South America, and halved the journey between San Francisco and New York from 22,500 km (14,000 miles) to 9,500 km (6,000 miles).

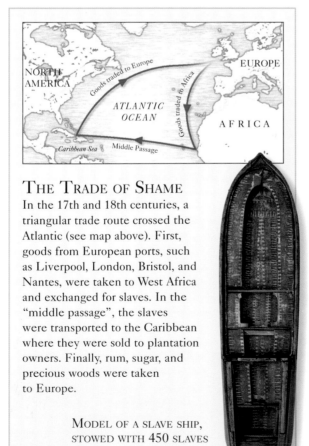

THE TRADE OF SHAME
In the 17th and 18th centuries, a triangular trade route crossed the Atlantic (see map above). First, goods from European ports, such as Liverpool, London, Bristol, and Nantes, were taken to West Africa and exchanged for slaves. In the "middle passage", the slaves were transported to the Caribbean where they were sold to plantation owners. Finally, rum, sugar, and precious woods were taken to Europe.

MODEL OF A SLAVE SHIP, STOWED WITH 450 SLAVES

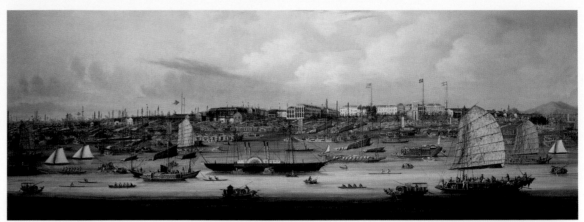

THE TEA TRADE
Until the middle of the 19th century, China was closed to trade with the outside world. One of the first ports to trade regularly with Europe was Canton (now Guangzhou), and it soon became the capital of China's tea trade with Europe. This painting shows the Pearl River at Canton, busy with local junks and the Hong Kong steamship.

BUNDLES OF TEA

PIRAEUS The largest port in Greece is Piraeus, the port of Athens. It was built in the 5th century BCE around a natural deep harbour, and was fortified with walls to protect the Athenian fleet. But, in 396 CE, the port was destroyed and abandoned until the 19th century, when Athens became the Greek capital.

QUEBEC One of the first European settlements in Canada, Quebec became the centre of the fur trade. Colonized by the French in 1608, the French and English fought over Quebec many times. Today, it is the heart of French Canada.

ROTTERDAM The largest port in Europe and one of the most modern in the world, Rotterdam is situated at the mouth of the River Rhine in Holland. It is linked to the sea by a canal large enough for ocean-going ships.

SINGAPORE The port of Singapore, in Southeast Asia, has been a trading centre since the 14th century. In the 19th century, Singapore was controlled by the British and the East India Company. It grew rapidly as trade developed with merchants from Malaysia and China. Today, Singapore is one of the biggest ports in the world and a major international financial centre.

ST PETERSBURG St Petersburg was founded in 1703 by the Russian tsar, Peter the Great. He built it as a naval base and as a port for trade in the Baltic. It soon became an industrial and cultural centre and Russia's leading seaport.

SUEZ CANAL The Suez Canal in Egypt links the Mediterranean Sea with the Red Sea and the Indian Ocean. It is 160 km (100 miles) long and took 10 years to build. It was opened in 1869 and made a huge impact on world trade, cutting the distance between London and Bombay (now Mumbai) by 7,125 km (4,425 miles).

VENICE Venice lies on a network of canals and lagoons in northeast Italy. It became a trading city between the 9th and the 11th centuries, and soon dominated the eastern Mediterranean Sea. By the 13th century, it had become a great sea power, together with its rival city, Genoa, on the other side of Italy. Its power declined in the 15th century with the discovery of America and sea routes to Asia.

YOKOHAMA The port of Yokohama in Japan only opened up to trade with foreign countries in 1859. It became the centre for trade with Japan, and was famous for the export of silk.

SHIPPING THROUGH THE AGES

The story of ships began thousands of years ago, when people realized that they could cross water using a log. Rafts and dugout canoes with paddles followed, then boats of wooden planks, and the use of oars. Next, sails were used, at first only if the wind was blowing in the right direction, but then a zigzagging technique, called tacking, was discovered, and sails could be used wherever the wind blew.

REED BOAT
Where there was no timber, people made boats from other materials. This reed boat is from Lake Titicaca, high in the Andes mountains of South America, where trees do not grow.

BIRCHBARK CANOE
Some people made canoes and boats by constructing a wooden frame and stretching animal hides or strips of bark over it to make light, waterproof craft. This birchbark canoe was made by the Algonquin – a Native American tribe from Ontario, Canada.

POLYNESIAN OUTRIGGER
The Polynesians were expert sailors who originally came from Southeast Asia. They sailed all over the Pacific Ocean, in light catamarans (boats with two hulls) and outriggers (boats with a wooden float fitted to the hull), discovering and colonizing islands.

EGYPTIAN SHIP
From c. 3000 BCE, the Egyptians used imported wood to build strong seagoing ships with sails and oars for rowing and steering.

DOVER BOAT
Remains of a boat from c. 1500 BCE shows early boats were built with planks in Northern Europe, as well as in the Mediterranean.

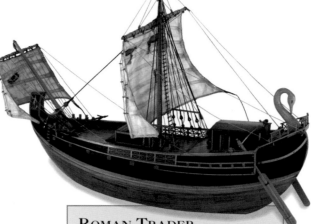

ROMAN TRADER
Roman trading ships sailed all around the Empire. This big barge, dating from c. 200 CE, was used to bring grain from Egypt to Rome.

CHINESE JUNK
Chinese junks sailed the seas from the 5th or 6th centuries. They were used to explore Africa's East coast until the early 1400s, when Chinese Emperors cut off all contact with foreigners.

VIKING KNORR
This Viking trader dates from the 11th century and was wider than a longship. The nautical term "starboard" comes from the steering oar or "steerboard", which was always on the right-hand side.

VENETIAN GALLEY
From around 1200 until 1700, countries around the Mediterranean favoured galleys for both trading and military purposes. This painting shows Venetian war galleys.

A TIMELINE OF SHIPPING

Egyptian Ship

3000   2500   2000   1500 Dover Boat

GREEK TRADER
Greek galleys sailed the Mediterranean from c. 800 BCE. Traders usually had sails and one level of oars. Warships, such as the trireme, were powered by 170 oarsmen who sat in three levels.

ARAB DHOW
Since the 8th century, and probably earlier, Arab dhows with triangular lateen sails have crossed the Red Sea, Indian Ocean, and Persian Gulf, trading goods between continents.

COG
This 14th-century Northern-European vessel had a square sail and a central rudder, which became standard in all ocean-going ships.

CARAVEL
In the 15th century, the Portuguese sailed caravels in their search for a passage around Africa to India. Two of the ships that Columbus used to sail to America in 1492 were caravels.

EAST INDIAMAN
The largest ships of the 18th and 19th centuries, East Indiamen carried passengers and cargo, but could also fight. Dividing the sails into several smaller ones meant they could be handled by a smaller crew.

PASSENGER LINER
From the late 19th century to the 1930s, shipping companies competed to produce the fastest, most luxurious liners. In 1906, the *Mauretania*, above, was the star liner of the Cunard Line.

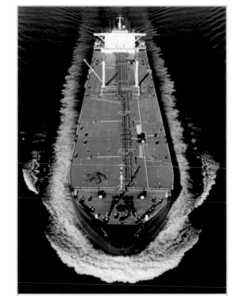

CARRACK
The carrack of the 15th century was an important advance in ship design. Square sails and three masts gave it manoeuvrability. It also had raised constructions, called castles, at the front and back.

CLIPPER
The fastest sailing ships of the mid-19th century were the clippers that raced to China, bringing tea back to Europe. With its large sail area and narrow hull, a clipper could cover 500 km (310 miles) in a day.

OIL TANKER
In the 1950s and 60s, ever-larger oil tankers were designed to meet the growing demand for oil. The largest tankers today are often more than 450 m (1,500 ft) long.

CONTAINER SHIP
Since the 1950s, much of the world's cargo has been transported in standard-size containers, which can be lifted on and off giant ships and lorries by cranes.

Greek Trader | 500 | Roman Trader 200 | Chinese Junk 400 | Arab Dhow 700 | Viking Knorr 1000 | Venetian Galley 1200 | Cog 1300 | Caravel 1400 | Carrack | Galleon 1600 | East Indiaman 1700 | Clipper Steamship 1800 | Passenger Liner Oil Tanker Container Ship 1900 | Queen Mary 2 2000

BCE 0 CE 100 300 500 600 800 900 1100 1500

GALLEON
Developed from the carrack, a galleon was a square-sailed, three-masted sailing ship that crossed the seas from the 16th to 17th centuries. It could be a formidable fighting ship and was particularly popular with the Spanish navy.

STEAMSHIP
In the 19th century, the introduction of steam power and the use of iron changed the design of trading and fighting ships. In 1838, the *Great Western* (right) was the first ship to cross the Atlantic using steam power.

QUEEN MARY 2
As cruise holidays become ever more popular, shipping companies are building new, bigger liners. The *Queen Mary 2*, launched in 2004, can carry 2,620 passengers and 1,253 crew.

WHERE IS HE?

Did you spot the accident-prone characters in red, yellow, and green getting into trouble over the centuries? Check below that you found the right man.

PAGES 4-5
He's caught a crab ...   chasing a goose ...   stubbing his toe ...   and falling off the quay.

PAGE 6
He's knocked over a pile of ivory.

PAGE 8
A goat has spotted him behind the jewellery smith.

PAGE 11
He's getting a beating outside the inn.

PAGE 12
The travelling dentist has him in his clutches.

PAGE 15
He's managed to get his foot stuck in a bucket.

PAGE 17
He's holding on tight at the top of the slave ship.

PAGE 18
He's the man who's feeling very seasick.

PAGE 21
Did you spot him under the table in the tavern?

PAGE 23
He's about to get doused with wet paint!

PAGE 25
He's managed to get caught up in a deckchair.

PAGE 27
He's in trouble again, this time with the police.

INDEX

Index: Sylvia Potter
Maps: Ed Merrit

The publisher would like to thank the following for their kind permission to reproduce their photographs:
(Key: a-above; b-below/bottom; c-centre; f-far; l-left; r-right; t-top)
akg-images: 30frb; Peter Connolly 30bc. **Alamy Images:** Kos Picture Source 31fcr; Peter Titmuss 31br. **The Art Archive:** Museo Correr Venice/Dagli Orti (A) 30fcr; Dagli Orti 30tc; Eileen Tweedy 31bc. The Trustees of the British Museum; 5ftl, 5tl; **Corbis:** 29fcla; Joel W. Rogers 31bl. **DK Images:**

Exeter Maritime Museum, The National Maritime Museum, London 30fcla, 30fcl, 30ftr; International Sailing Craft Association, Lowestoft 30bl; National Maritime Museum, London 29fcra, 30cr, 30fbr, 30br, 31clb, 31ftr, 31fl; Wilberforce House Museum, Hull 29bc. **Dover Museum:** The Dover Bronze Age Boat Trust 30c. **Getty Images:** Workbook Stock 31cr. **Michael Holford:** 30tr. **Mary Evans Picture Library:** 31fcl. **National Maritime Museum, London:** 29tr, 31cla.

All other images © Dorling Kindersley
For further information see: www.dkimages.com

CREDITS